"Ira Rat writes raw, like no one will ever read this, but I did and I cried. It's like being let down by someone when you really need them, or perhaps put down or abandoned, left to reconcile loneliness with some more general despair, settling for quiescence because contentment is out of reach or something only meant for others."

— Charlene Elsby (author, *The Devil Thinks I'm Pretty* & *Violent Faculties*)

"Picture a tiny pastel heart-shaped conversation candy briefly savored then spat into a sandbox; its washed-out frontal surface bearing the vague bothersome inscription: What Has Been Will Be Again."

— Evan Isoline (author, *Philosophy of the Sky* & *Deadmath*)

Endless Now
Copyright © 2023 Ira Rat
Book & cover design by Ira Rat

This is a work of fiction. Names, characters, businesses, places, events, locales, and incidents are either the products of the author's imagination or used in a fictitious manner. Any resemblance to actual persons, living or dead, or actual events is purely coincidental.

This book may not be reproduced in whole or in part, except for the inclusion of brief quotations in a review, without permission in writing from the author or publisher. No part of this publication may be reproduced, stored in or introduced into retrieval system, or transmitted, in any form, or by any means (electronic, mechanical, photocopying, recording, or otherwise), without prior permission of the publisher.

Requests for permission should be directed to eyerarat@gmail.com

FIRST EDITION

ENDLESS NOW IRA RAT

Filthy Loot

filthyloot.com

ALSO BY IRA RAT

Fiction
Pacifier (stories)
Participation Trophy

Non-Fiction
a beginner's guide to extreme horror (with Jon Steffens)

Poetry
Juvenilia
The Medication
Bitter

Art
i'm sorry mom
inspiration is theft

Edited by
Teenage Grave
Isolation is Safety
Little Birds

FOR EMILY

Special Thanks: Elle Nash, Nate Lippens,
Jon Steffens, Thomas Moore, Shane Jesse Christmass,
Charlene Elsby, & Sam Richard,
all for different reasons.

the heart is an anxious muscle

What is it
I'm trying to say?
Your guess is
a cliché I'll endlessly
repeat

The sentimentality
of vacuousness

The nostalgia
of terrors you thought
that you burned
away with
endless nights
at the bottle

Writing pithy words
by the blue light
of my phone.

Like licking dirt
from a bully's
outstretched fingers

the act of being polite

I try to disappear as
People make idle chit-chat,
a few decibels too loud
to not be a distraction
my skin bristles at their
general pleasantries

sink into
the backdrop/
will
myself deaf

but all they're trying
to be is "nice"
While I try to be
something other than
here

the euclidean geometry of not giving a fuck

I would
appreciate some
social sadism

Tell me how ugly
I am / while
Ripping out
My hair

Tell me to
never show
my face again
with the polite
smile of a
Midwesterner

The world
is spinning
But nobody
notices
Because
that's the way it's
always been.

an anticipation greater than reality

Every time I put down a word
I feel the unsufferable weight
of expectation, not from *you*
nobody would give a fuck if
I never wrote another word.

The sink drips, how pathetically
poetical is that?

I'm just waiting for a the sign
that was promised me from
the Technicolor world
behind the screen,
I don't speak to myself
other than in riddles
hints from my unconscious
that this insufferable weight
is my own

drip

I play surrealist parlor games
with my brain
a Freudian analysis
of watching myself
write about nothing
a Kobayashian ouroboros
of meaninglessness
anxiety dulls my wits
The sound of my sink dripping
goes on forever
nothing happens.

insignificance

I don't like this feeling
as much as I would
have thought
the walls are closing
on me, I'm closing in
on myself. the world
is getting so small
that it can't be seen.
I try to put into words
but they fail me
—and I them
it starts again
each time a little
tighter, a little
smaller, a little
more insignificant

memory: trailer park (high school)

The haze from half-a-dozen dangling cigarettes had begun to obscure the mosaic of scotch-taped centerfolds that gridded the ceiling.

Of the smokers, half were watching a hazily shot VHS porno of two women going at it, that some one had pocketed last week from the mom-and-pop video store off the highway that ran through the middle of town, isolating the trailer park.

The lazily erotic shot through the gauze of a Vaselined lens.

The others were playing Magic on an unmade bed, hustling each other for cards with fantasy novel creatures, worth more than their parent's rent.

The room, a shack-like addition, vibrated to the sounds of 80s metal and loud voices—reeking of ditch weed, locker room, and desperation for something to happen.

the end of every fork

i helped my corporation prey
upon the weak, stupid, and poor
and i don't think have license
to be poetic about that
it was my job to separate fools
from their money
to make sure that they continue
to swim in the debt that
we created for them
i could joke about that, but i
probably shouldn't
if i want to retain any of the —
albeit minimal — respect given to me
by my peers
i am a monster with a toothy grin
and no sense of shame
over what filled my dinner plate
sometimes i wonder if my lack of remorse
should be more troubling
but it's not.

better all the time

I'm staring at
the walls again
not bragging
it's just what I do

Time feels like its
moving so fast that
it has left
me paralyzed

if I were to have
dreams again
I would want
to dream of
of floating

But when I close
my eyes, I just get
seven hours of darkness
that feel like 10 minutes

If I weren't so humble
I might gloat that I
feel broken in a novel way.
but I fear I'm getting
better all the time

a low hum

Jessie's hand wrapped around his Juul like he was pulling some sleight of hand. Disappearing and reappearing only for the briefest of flashes preceding huge plumes of opaque steam.

"Yeah, I really used to like going to shows. Now all I can think about is if I'm facilitating sex criminals as they hop from state to state, fucking their way to cancellation."

His voice starts fading away into the low hum of willed-tinnitus.

endless now

I don't
think any
of it is
helping
like they
said it
would

I still
feel nauseous
most of the
time and
the pills
aren't helping
this anxiety,
my hand
shakes for
no reason,
and my eyes
see four
of everything

the pills
to help
the pills
are getting

into the
double digits
and time
keeps melting
away like
a chemtrail
behind me

I asked
if I could
stop
they said
no

now
is an
endless
now
is an
endless
now
is endless

I sleep
but I
don't rest,
My eyes
are closed
but there

are no
dreams

entropy
always
wins

anxiety
without
limit

The pamphlet says
to write down your
desires, re-read
them every day
re-write them as
needed
re-want them
every waking
moment
re-arrange your
life to only want,
become a wanting
machine,
and maybe you'll
just get the things
that you want
after all
but they never

mention
when to stop
or how

I make
analogs
of things
in my life
to things
that happened
to family
that are
no longer
here,
like
when they
didn't tell
me my
mother was
dying until
she was
in hospice,
clean white
sheets
no heart
monitor
just a
drugged
peace

until
nothing.
is there
something
they're not
telling me?

(cough)

my knees hurt
from praying
though I haven't
been to church
since I was six
I don't even
know if I believed
then, so maybe
I'm just begging

now
is endless,
perpetually
nostalgic
for things
that never
happened
or will
happen
or ever

could
happen
past is
now
future
now
/now
never
existed

I don't
exist
my life
a figment
of my own
devising

Last night I thought that I would die if I fell asleep. I sat dizzy and emotionless to the thought of this finally being my time. On TV the judges agreed that all the chefs were equal and they went onto the next round. I waited and it passed. I told the doctor, but they didn't think it was anything.

i'm sorry mom

My mom used
to take me to
work with her
when I was 11
or so,
so that I could
explore the big(ger)
city during the
weekends.
recently I
realized that
she was letting
me off 2 minutes
from where
Johnny Gosche
got kidnapped
years before.
it's not like
she didn't know,
she mentioned
him often enough,
during meals, watching
tv, teaching me
to tie my shoes,

it was
like she was
using The Secret
in order to manifest
my disappearance.
but I always came
back, and for that,
i'm sorry mom

i cough

I cough, trying

to pass yards

of cheesecloth

ectoplasmic

chicanery

of fake ghosts

my coughs

are table raps

I slept all morning

but I still feel

like I'm being pulled

through the

floor

The highs are gone

and the lows keep

diving

I don't even see

the middle from

here

The pills are getting smaller

I've got words to

describe the feeling

I could even play MadLibs

with the adjectives

but none of them

my own,

and none of them are

right.

The birds chirp too loud

and the mailman calls

someone a "motherfucker"

I'm inside the dark

hiding from the other shadows

metal chimes outside

pitch-perfect to a song

about murder

I haven't felt right

in so long that

I've forgot its taste

I call the clinic

to let them know

the pills aren't working

again

I call the clinic

to let them know

the pills aren't working

again

I call the clinic

to let them know

the pills aren't working

I don't believe the tests.

Blinding headaches, nausea

sleeping through the day

gaining weight, getting pulled

through the floor

aging a year every day

like time-lapse photography

wrinkles appearing, hair

gray then gone,

my knees give out

from below

They hold specialists over my head

like the last man in hell with a chance

of redemption

If certain animals stop chewing

their teeth will keep growing

until they can't open

their mouths

10-hours in a car,

just for a few stops,

stop at another infected hotel

they say it's not

but they all are

two beds, one for the cliche

of who I used to be.

It's always too dark to sleep

I don't even see

the shadows on

the walls

what cliche is left to flog

that hasn't been done to death?

a fire took out all my work

don't know if it's worth rebuilding

or I'm doing it out of habit,

another cliche

So I watch bootleg

art films, with the

blinds drawn, pretending

meaning when there is

none

a man mumbles

(cuts back)

he mumbles again

(a third time)

each a little less

coherent than the

last

Alone in the soupy gray

of a hotel pool

just my eyes above water

I'm sure it's time to leave

but I don't know how

eighth grade

In eighth grade, our house burned down
The same week, my father had a heart attack.
& lost his leg to sudden diabetes
I missed my childhood toys more
than I missed his ability to walk
Now that he's gone,
lung cancer, this time
I miss the toys that he gave me
More than I miss him.

evan

The rumor was that Evan had walked up to the highway last week and had finally climbed into the first car that would stop for him – with no plan or destination in mind.

I don't know how he was surviving; he certainly didn't have any money when he left. No one did. Not around here.

But as someone suggested, if he had a mouth, and an ass – there were always ways for enterprising sixteen-year-olds to make money on the road.

Digging through the ashtray, I find one with a few drags left in it. Straightening it out, I light it and blow out a cloud of blue-gray smoke.

I'm not even sure if it mattered to him if he survived. As long as he didn't die here.

Evan told me once that his biggest fear was never leaving the trailer park. Until that night he never had, other than to go a block in either direction to go to school, or the convenience store.

Mango Cherry

From outside of a claustrophobically small bathroom, we hear dull and repetitive party music muffled to the point where it's mostly a thud, thud, thud. Underscoring the conversation between NICK and WARREN.

Both NICK and WARREN are in their mid-20s. NICK sits on the toilet, though not using it. WARREN stands at the mirror primping, making sure that he's looking flawless. At points, he even pulls out a toothbrush and starts absently dry brushing his teeth.

NICK: I had a dream about you last night…

WARREN: Ugh, don't tell me about it. I hate hearing about people's dreams. Even… especially… if they include me. *It's just too telling.*

I really have no desire to have a look into other people's psyches. It's unnerving, like sending me an unsolicited link to your OnlyFans account.

NICK: It's nothing like that…

WARREN: Says you, I'm too much of an armchair psychologist *not* to read into it. It's uncomfortable. So, sorry… but this is a hard pass from me.

NICK: ...*ok.*

WARREN: Don't turn all passive-aggressive on me. Would you prefer me sitting here silently resenting you, as you're doing a striptease of your thoughts in front of me?

NICK: I said, it's not...

WARREN: ... like that, I know. I'd have even more questions about your sanity, or your lack thereof if you were having sex dreams about me. I just don't feel comfortable being that intimate with anyone, let alone you. No offense.

NICK: Are you really that shallow that you think that just because you were in it, it has anything to do with you?

WARREN: Again, I know that it has nothing to do with me, other than the way that it makes me feel. If you were to suddenly whip out your prick and started waving it around. It would make me feel the same way. Uncomfortable, and slightly embarrassed for *you*.

Knock on the door, both NICK and WARREN sit in silence waiting for it to pass, with the gravity of people waiting for the bombers to pass overhead in a WWII movie.

OUTSIDE VOICE: Quit sucking each other off in there!

WARREN (shouting): We've only got a couple more lines, give us a minute.

NICK (surprised, whispering): You've got…?

WARREN raises his finger to his mouth while subtly shaking his head "no"

OUTSIDE VOICE (calmer): Can I…

NICK and WARREN (in unison, loud but not angry): No.

WARREN: We've only got a little bit, sorry, maybe next time.

NICK and WARREN share a pregnant silence waiting for a response that never comes. After several seconds, they relax their postures and go back to how they were before.

NICK: Was that Frankie?

WARREN: Sounded like him.

NICK: I thought he was…

WARREN: From what I heard they let him go, the police said the video was from the internet, so they couldn't prove she was under 18.

NICK: Well, that's comforting. Need to get Chris Maloney on that shit.

WARREN: (Mimics the *Law and Order* sound) *Ba Bom*! Apparently, there are companies online that make perfectly legal movies for freaks like him. Have you seen his girlfriend? He *obviously* has a type. Unfortunately, that type is girls who look twelve.

NICK: Sick shit.

WARREN: The sickest.

NICK continues to stare off into the distance, and WARREN resumes checking himself out in the mirror.

WARREN: Speaking of sick, (points to a spot on his neck) does this look like a goiter?

NICK: What?

WARREN (gives a dismissive wave): Nothing, joke. I forgot that you were a *French* Lit major.

NICK: Oookay.

WARREN: I've got to take a leak.

NICK gets off the toilet and passes WARREN the space is slightly too small for this to be done with any grace or elegance, first trying to pass each other crotch-to-crotch, then ass-to-ass, finally settling on crotch-to-ass. NICK turns to face the door, as WARREN starts a rather long piss that takes an extended period of time to finish. They continue talking throughout.

WARREN (a little louder to be heard over his urinating): Beckett.

NICK: What?

WARREN (a little quieter): I was quoting, or rather misquoting Godot… Because we're in here, waiting…

NICK give the door an "oh…" face, that WARREN doesn't see.

WARREN (still adjusting his volume) Something about "looks like a goiter". I don't know, the line always stuck out to me because you don't hear the term "goiter" very often.

NICK: We're waiting for something?

WARREN: I don't know if we're waiting for *something*, (finishes) but we're not doing anything either. (pauses) Excuse me.

WARREN and NICK do their little dance again, and WARREN is once again primping in front of the mirror, having not washed his hands. NICK closes and flushes the toilet, and once again sits back down.

NICK: Do you believe in aliens?

WARREN: What? I mean it's a statistical…

NICK: No, I mean right here and now on this planet.

WARREN (a little offput): Uhhh… Are you a closet Q or something?

NICK: No, that dream I was talking about earlier.

WARREN makes a *not this shit again* face.

NICK: It was this *exact* situation. Same conversation, same everything.

WARREN looks at NICK like he's gone off the deep end, and imperceptibly starts inching away, as much as the lack of room will allow.

WARREN: Ohhhkay?

NICK: This is the part where you started telling me that you were an alien and started saying weird shit about how the world was going to end shortly.

WARREN: Well, I'm not, and I don't think it is.

Outside the music that has been going steady suddenly stops. A new song doesn't start. NICK and WARREN remain in silence for a half-beat longer than is comfortable. They both look worried.

NICK (whispers): Is the party over?

WARREN (mimics NICK's volume): I don't know. Sounds that way. Though I don't hear anyone leaving. Do you think the cops came?

NICK: In this neighborhood?

WARREN: Yeah… *They* seem like the kind of people who would have made sure that nobody around here would have called in a complaint.

NICK and WARREN stare at each other, as if they were trying to will the other one to do something, for an uncomfortably long time.

NICK: Do you think the world has ended?

WARREN (Voice and demeanor wavering, and unsure of himself for the first time): Don't be ridiculous.

NICK: Then *you* open the door.

WARREN stares at the doorknob.

Suddenly the music starts again.

NICK: Shiiiit. OK. Should we make an appearance now?

WARREN (Looks down at his feet): Maybe later.

FILTHY LOOT
"MISFIT FICTIONS"
AMES IA | EST. 2018

FILTHY LOOT is an independent press, based out of Ames, IA. Focused on misfit fictions and odd other ideas — we publish books, zines and assorted miscellany in both open and limited edition formats.

TALENTED PERVERTS™ is an imprint of Filthy Loot, focusing on "aesthetic fiction," poetry, and art.

- ☐ *a beginner's guide to extreme horror* by Jon Steffens & Ira Rat
- ☐ *Dirt in the Sky* (Anthology)
- ☐ *Hollow Coin* by S.T. Cartledge
- ☐ *Isolation is Safety* (Anthology)
- ☐ *LAZERMALL* (Anthology)
- ☐ *Letters to Jenny Just After She Died* by Charlene Elsby ‡
- ☐ *Little Birds* (Anthology)
- ☐ *METH-DTF.* by Shane Jesse Christmass ‡
- ☐ *My Mind is Not a Billboard//What's Your Favorite TV Show?* by Sam Pink
- ☐ *Pacifier* by Ira Rat
- ☐ *Participation Trophy* by Ira Rat
- ☐ *Shagging the Boss* by Rebecca Rowland
- ☐ *Teenage Grave* (Anthology)
- ☐ *The Doom that Came To Mellonville* by Madison McSweeny
- ☐ *The God in the Hills and Other Horrors* by Jon Steffens
- ☐ *The Medication* by Ira Rat ‡
- ☐ *The Vine that Ate the Starlet* by Madeleine Swann
- ☐ *Wax and Wane* by Saoirse Ní Chiaragáin

‡ **TALENTED PERVERTS ™**

www.ingramcontent.com/pod-product-compliance
Lightning Source LLC
LaVergne TN
LVHW092101060526
838201LV00047B/1506